T0151299

The Diving Bell

poems by
Elena Ignatova

translated from Russian by
SIBELAN FORRESTER

ZEPHYR PRESS
Brookline, MA

Cover art by Mikhail Naumtsev
Book design by *typeslowly*
Printed by Cushing-Malloy, Inc.

Zephyr Press acknowledges with gratitude the financial support
of the Massachusetts Cultural Council and the National Endowment
for the Arts.

NATIONAL
ENDOWMENT
FOR THE ARTS

massculturalcouncil.org

Library of Congress Cataloging-in-Publication Data

Ignatova, Elena.
   [Poems. English and Russian. Selections]
   The diving bell : poems / by Elena Ignatova ; translated from Russian by
Sibelan Forrester.
      p. cm.
   Poems in Russian and English translation.
   Includes bibliographical references and index.
   ISBN 0-939010-85-2 (alk. paper)
   1. Ignatova, Elena--Translations into English. I. Forrester, Sibelan E. S.
(Sibelan Elizabeth S.) II. Title.
   PG3482.G637A2 2006
   891.71'5--dc22

                                             2006011972

98765432 first edition in 2006

ZEPHYR PRESS
50 Kenwood Street
Brookline, MA 02446
www.zephyrpress.org

Table of Contents

Introduction

Elena Ignatova's poetry works to protect her readers and herself in a hostile, often toxic environment. It offers ways to approach and understand experience, even as it reflects the flaws and compromises of human beings in an imperfect world.

Ignatova draws attention to the tragic disharmony between how things should be and how they are: the dark side of Russian history from the days of Prince Igor and the Mongol invasions, through the *oprichniki* (gang of armed bodyguards) of Ivan the Terrible, to the Revolution, the Second World War, and the breakdowns and difficulties she has witnessed in her own lifetime. Her language mobilizes Soviet officialese and conversational vocabulary, along with remnants of old poetic solemnity, religious, official and folk locutions. And religion for Ignatova plays a role like poetry's: it is a source of rigor and epiphany that makes her poetic speaker uncompromisingly self-critical but also may enable a burst of joy or hope against a depressing background. She doesn't force her religion on her reader, but it is strongly present—a Russian Orthodox or Biblical cultural undertone with residues of folk belief, an inevitable and essential part of the landscape, and deeply felt personal experience.

Elena Alekseevna Ignatova was born in Leningrad in 1947. Her family, as she comments, had no particular tradition of reading poetry. She spent a good part of her childhood with grandparents in a Russian village near Smolensk, a setting that informs many of her poems. By her teens she had begun to seek out other poets and writers in Leningrad;

including the aged Anna Akhmatova, whom she described as stately and imposing as Catherine the Great. In *Dangerous Acquaintances*, her memoir about Sergei Dovlatov, Ignatova writes, "I recall with gratitude the literary atmosphere of the 1960s, with its harsh division into good and bad, decent and indecent, with its stubborn refusal to accept everything that was of the alien mentality."

Ignatova was not much younger than the best-known "Leningrad poets," Joseph Brodsky and his circle, but those few years made a crucial difference in her experience. Her self-image as a poet formed in the stimulating atmosphere of the Khrushchev-era "Thaw," and, like many of her peers, she remained true to her literary ideals as she came of age and Soviet culture settled into Brezhnev-era stagnation. Ignatova became an artistic dissident against the hopelessly compromised literary establishment, though she never joined the more alienated literary "underground." She had graduated with a degree in Philology from Leningrad State University and lectured there in Russian philology until 1979. Her first publication was in the journal *Смена* ('Shift') in 1963, but after 1968 she published mostly abroad and in *samizdat*—the unofficial, usually hand- or typewritten, self-publishing system that made so much literature available to those Soviet citizens lucky enough to live in the metropolis and willing to risk spending time with potentially dangerous manuscripts. Her friends included other disaffected writers; she has written with particular affection about her friendship with Venedikt Erofeev.

In 1975 Ignatova first published a poem abroad, in so-called *tamizdat*, and her first book of poems, *Стихи о причастности* ('Verses about Belonging'), appeared in Paris the following year, with the obligatory editorial note that it was being published without the author's knowledge or approval. Two collections came out later in samizdat: *Здесь, где живу* ('Here where I live,' 1983), and *Стихотворения* ('Poems,' 1985). The opening of the Russian literary scene under *glasnost* gave her new access to readers and recognition as a writer. Her first and last "official" Soviet book, *Теплая земля* ('The Warm Earth,' 1989), came out from the prestigious "Soviet Writer" publishing house in Leningrad. During these years she also wrote screenplays for literary documentaries on Akhmatova, Blok and Bely.

In 1990 Ignatova and her family moved to Israel, not long be-

[x]

fore her native city's name was changed back to St. Petersburg. She published *Небесное зарево* ('Celestial Glow') in Jerusalem in 1992. However, her native city has always been present in her writing, and she "returned" in 1997 with the substantial historical and cultural survey *Записки о Петербурге* ('Notes on St. Petersburg'), which she revised and expanded in a second edition in time for the city's 300th anniversary. Here she intersperses her own experiences and urban family connections with citations from famous Russian writers and 19th-century and earlier memoirs. The book traces deep layers of history and memory: Ignatova's Petersburg is a palimpsest city. She notes in the introduction, "I wrote this book because I was looking for answers to questions that are important for our time, but mainly because I wanted to look into the past of Petersburg, into its ordinary life, to feel the breath and warmth of this departed life, to hear the voices of people from earlier generations. And to understand better the meaning of the gift we have received—a surprising city, our common link with its destiny." Her most recent collection of poetry, *Избранное*, was published in Jerusalem in 2005.

The Diving Bell presents a small part of Ignatova's work, but aims to trace her most urgent themes. Along with the beauties and chimeras of Leningrad/St. Petersburg, she describes other parts of the Russian Empire or Soviet Union, Lithuania, Crimea, or the steppe, rural Smolensk and the woods of the far North, dotted with relics of labor camps. More recent treatments of émigré experience may recall the loss of pre-Revolutionary Russian culture in some of her earlier poems. Ignatova does not date her poems, though sometimes dates are implied by topics like Chernobyl or Saddam Hussein's soldiers in the first Gulf War. When she points to an era more specifically, it is often the "nature preserve" of childhood in the 1950s, a time whose pleasures and beauties become troubled in the adult's more informed recollection. Classical culture, history and mythology appear, as befits a philologist:

> You can spend a century reading Herodotus:
> Scythians beat Persians, then the Persians burn someone …
> But the bloodstains fade. In your history are
> the rustle of olives, the peasant smell of sweat.

The coarse clan of the Greeks grows pettier,
the naval vessel hastens towards Egypt.
We cannot drink up all of a stranger's grief,
we see just names, like stubble after reaping,
and the walking-staff beat out on these lands' stone.

And where is it, land of the arrogant Lydians,
gold-bearing rivers and golden linen sails,
where the world's in embryo, where it's still so dense,
where the blood of burned cities walks around the sky,
where man is cruel and naked and free of care ...

Other poems cite Ovid, the exile so important to Pushkin and
Mandelstam, two Russian poets who could not travel freely but com-
pensated for that with the imaginative power of their writing. Ignatova's
more recent poetry is set in Israel, especially Jerusalem where she now
lives, and treats both émigré sorrows (loss of ties of friendship and
residence, erosion of memory, and unwitting, even unwilling changes
in the poet's self and perceptions) and the local combination of beauty
and violence that is, ultimately, another form of things she had expe-
rienced earlier in Russia.

The poems are full of plants, trees, sun, and water. Ignatova's land-
scape embodies nature and culture, clouds over a granite embankment,
a marching band reflected in rainy pavement. Her Leningrad verses are
often set in a park, full of visible signs of past history, crystallizing that
city's poetic life for the delight and refinement of human beings. The
poems are also marked by economy. It is a truism that Russian sentences
will be longer than their English equivalents, and this is true of many
of Ignatova's lines, but not all. Some are almost painfully spare, such as
"погост, где брат мой спит без снов" (from the third poem in the cycle
"And of Russian Verse ..."), a mere eight beats in seven words, which
I can render no more sparely than "a churchyard where my brother
sleeps dreamless," ten syllables that barely scan. Or, «Поэт со мной,
москвич с лицом изгоя»—a line of iambic pentameter that means,
literally, "the poet with me, a Muscovite with the face of an outcast."
The longest lines, such as "The harshest times can't force you to drink
down the drivel of humility," are still densely and tensely detailed.

Like Russian vodka, her verse is highly concentrated, infused with aromas, colors, bitter hints of what remains unsaid. Her tragic worldview often lingers on the scars of Russian history: the Revolution, Stalinism, the Second World War, or events in Israel. Critic Mikhail Kopeliovich comments, "Ignatova is primarily elegiac; harshness is more characteristic of her than lyrical relaxation," and this is true of both her form and her underlying philosophy. Words or motifs (mica; clouds; the titular diving bell itself) gain intensity through shifting contexts and changes in tone. Hers is a poetry of address, often citing an interlocutor so she can respond with an alternate view of events. The formal aspects as well as clear citations recall Derzhavin, Akhmatova, Mandelstam, Tsvetaeva, and Pushkin, yet the verse has an unmistakably contemporary stylistic range, colored by current events and dissident angst, the subversive linguistic play and conversational ease of the late Soviet period. Poems take shape in places where she has visited or has family ties (Crimea, Smolensk). Her work of the 1990s brings in the new, ancient environs of Jerusalem, described as crystalline, distinct from St. Petersburg's characteristic granite, a more chaotically igneous material. Ignatova says, "I am convinced that art is active: it can reflect the destruction of the world, of the historical connections of eras, of the human soul—or, on the contrary, can strengthen those connections. I have always wanted to write about the internal connection, the harmony of the world even in difficult times, about the connection of the past with our own fates, about Russia, about the connections of spaces: of the world of the Russian village, where I passed my childhood, of St. Petersburg and the Holy Land." In their recurring images and concerns, her poems create similar webs of connection within this volume.

Readers and translators frequently comment on the persistence of what Russians call "classical" verse, meaning that it adheres more or less strictly to meters that became standard in the eighteenth and nineteenth centuries. In essence, it is poetry that rhymes, scans, and therefore feels old-fashioned to North American readers. I am not sure that the Russian language really does offer more rhymes than other European languages (Pushkin, at least, did not think so!), since the easy solution of rhyming grammatical endings would not be used by a self-respecting poet. Nonetheless, many of the available rhymes are not yet overused, and slant rhyme feels quite fresh in the hands of a poet like Ignatova. In a formal sense, at least, I might compare her verbal texture to Dylan Thomas's or Sylvia Plath's. As Daniel Weissbort has pointed out, the poets of the Silver Age exerted a "delayed influence" on more recent writers, as their uncensored work splashed onto the Russian literary scene only in the late 1980s. Even if many forbidden things were available to a young philologist in Leningrad in the 1960s and 1970s, they were banned from public discourse almost until the end of the Soviet period, when the Russian literary scene changed irrevocably. For some in Ignatova's generation, maintaining traditional meters offers a way to safeguard artistic integrity, to integrate and extend the humanistic tradition of the Modernists. Ignatova's earlier poetry tends to be formally looser and more experimental, while her mature work is more classical in this sense. Thus, her distinctive voice feels familiar, or better—*familial*—to a reader who is acquainted with her predecessors: she consciously lives up to their example in this and other ways.

In most cases I have not used completely free verse in rendering Ignatova's poetry. I tried to capture sense and shape by paying Peter and Paul simultaneously, aiming for literal accuracy in meaning with maximal re-creation of form, and letting each concern serve to correct the other. I have chosen slant rhymes (sometimes quite obliquely slanted, like "channel" and "magic," "braid" and "sweet," or "strolling" and "peculiar"), when I could without padding or distorting the syntax, and copious assonance within and among lines. The translations emphasize rhythm above all, the persistent pulse of each poem, usually with a meditative walking pace, *andante*. I hope these compromises, given the more laissez-faire atmosphere of contemporary poetry in English, will convey the feeling of a "classical" style without infuriating readers who can read and appreciate the original Russian.

This translation could not have been made without support and suggestions from others. Elena Alekseevna Ignatova generously gave me advice on selecting poems, sent texts of work not yet published in collections, and answered questions about words and ideas: she has been as thoughtful and spiritually present in e-mail as she is in her poetry. I owe many thanks to Jim Kates of Zephyr Press, who encouraged my interest in translating Ignatova for the 1999 volume *In the Grip of Strange*

Thoughts, for inviting me to undertake this project, and for responding to drafts with patient and nit-picking comments. I first read Ignatova's verse in 1990, when Arlene Forman loaned me the copy of *Теплая земля* she had brought back to Oberlin from Leningrad. I thank Mark Markish (Ieromonakh Makarii) for his sharp eye and high standards of English grammar, and for taking time from a tremendously busy schedule to read the translations in draft. Expert translator Draginja Ramadanski had several valuable comments on this introduction. I have profited from Marina Rojavin's refined sense of language and profound knowledge of Russian poetry and culture, and from Yelena Forrester's musical ear and literate English style. N. B. inspired me in this work, as in everything. Any remaining infelicities are mine alone.

Sibelan Forrester,
Swarthmore, PA
November 2005

Медногубая музыка осени. Бас-геликон
кружит медленным небом. И колеблем, осыпан листвою,
проплывает военный оркестр в мокром воздухе по-над землею,
чуть повыше дождя занесен, накренен.

Скажет музыка: «О-о-о ...»—и отступит фонтанов вода.
Так застыли тритоны, что губы у них леденеют—
не сомкнуть, не ответить оркестру. Он медленно реет,
медью призрачной греет ... Дрожит за плечами слюда.

Что ж, российский Версаль? Нам достались из той стороны
этот парк щегольской, да надрывное слово «блокада»,
и не кроны деревьев—голодные ребра войны,
не эоловы арфы, а песня смертей и надсада.

Сеет дождик ... и плачу. И с криком летит «метеор»
вдоль оставленных парков. Угрюмо спешат экскурсанты
мимо братской могилы фонтанов, каскадов, озер,
мимо музыки—вниз головой—растворенных дождем оркестрантов.

~

Brass-lipped music of autumn. The helicon-bass makes a circle
around the slow sky. And shaken, scattered with leaves,
the army band sails through the wet air over the earth,
just a little above the rain it sweeps along, at an angle.

The music says "Ohhhh …"—and the fountains' water withdraws.
The tritons have frozen in place, so their lips turn to ice—
they can't open, can't answer the band. It slowly winnows,
warms with its ghostly brass … Mica trembles behind their backs.

So, a Russian Versailles? It's from those parts we acquired
this dandified park, plus the tragic expression "blockade,"
and not the trees' crowns—the hungry ribs of war,
not Aeolian harps, but an anthem of deaths and of strain.

Light rain falls, and I cry. And shrieking, the hydrofoil flies
along abandoned parks. The day-trippers glumly make haste
past the mass grave of fountains, of waterfalls, of lakes,
past the music—head down—of the players dissolved in the rain.

Едва ли не с начала сентября
на парки опускается заря,
и чувствует озябнувший прохожий
проникновенье осени в гортань,
когда ее отстоянный янтарь
надолго поселяется под кожей.

Вся осень сгустком кажется одним,
а воздух в ней—основа. Недвижим,
вдыхается с медлительною болью.
И стягивает горло горький сок
небес, свисающих над кромкою лесов,
и неба полого, стоящего над полем.

Когда всю глубину его вберешь,
вороны обрываются с берез,
кричат протяжно, кружатся в истоме…
Но луч блеснет, и виден парк насквозь:
жемчужный, ветхий, барственная кость—
мерцающий на мокром черноземе.

∼

Almost from the onset of September
the glow of sunset settles on the parks,
and the chilled passerby can sense
how autumn penetrates our vocal cords,
while its precipitated amber
settles for a long stay beneath our skin.

All autumn seems to be a single clot,
and air is its foundation. Motionless,
we breathe it in with slowly moving pain.
And our throat draws in the bitter juice
of skies that lower above the forests' edge,
and the hollow sky that stands above the field.

When you take in the wholeness of its depth,
an avalanche of crows breaks from the birches,
they cry at length, they circle in exhaustion …
but one ray gleams, and all the park shows through:
pearly, run-down, an aristocratic bone,
glimmering on the damp black earth.

Лепки небрежной лицо, Евину глину
ты переносишь на холст—тление в тленье.
Годы теплом надышали эти морщины,
знаки старенья.
Сердца и нынче не жаль—на́ половину!
Время его добывает, скоро ли сманит?
Были повинны в любви, ею палимы …
Вечная память!
Наши тела по ночам—робкие свечи—
светятся, погружены в кожу дивана,
и бесконечна стоит, безветренна вечность,
не задувает …
И пока смерть молода, нас не хватилась,
чтобы в земле залатать узкие щели,
мимо портреты глядят, делают милость,
не узнавая творца, не замечая модели.

A careless sculpture's face, the clay of Eve
you transfer to canvas—smoldering into decay.
The years have breathed warmth into these wrinkles,
tokens of aging.
Even now I don't stint with my heart—here, take half!
Time claims it bit by bit, will it soon be trapped?
We were culpable in love, seared by it.
Rest in peace!
Our bodies in the night—timid candles—
give off light, deep in the leather of the sofa,
and there is an endless, windless eternity,
it won't blow us out …
And while death's young yet, hasn't snatched us
to patch the narrow crevices in the earth,
the portraits glance past, they do us the favor,
not recognizing the artist, not noting the model.

~

Этот грустный и прекрасный мир.
Легким облаком накрытый день.
Только ангел над Невой летит,
серебристую роняя тень.

Слюдяное шелестенье крыл,
шестикрылое качанье плеч.
Только облако в Неве лежит,
не давая остывать и течь.

Воздух млечен. В нем слюда дрожит.
Затаился обнаженный свет.
Что на сердце за печаль, скажи?
Не любовь, о, не любовь, о, нет …

~

This sorrowful and splendid world.
The day is covered with light cloud.
Only an angel flies over the Neva,
casting a silvery shadow.

The micaceous rustling of wings,
six-winged swaying of shoulders.
Only a cloud lies within the Neva,
not allowing it to cool and flow.

The air is milky. Mica shakes in it.
The undressed light has hidden itself away.
Tell me, what is this sadness in my heart?
Not love, oh not love, oh no …

Памяти друга

1

Смерть—домовитая ласточка. Каждому сору и мимо—
летящему трепету крылышек—ведает место и вкус.
Тоньше соломинки ставший любимый
ею настигнут и спрятан в сияющий, плачущий куст,
в страшном гнезде предрождественской муки хранимый …
Я не увижу ни глаз его больше, ни уст.

Я ли бессмертье сулила? И на траве в Подмосковье
помню разрез удивленный глаза и радужной—тьму …
«Любишь?»—начавшись, записка кончалась: «с любовью»,
замкнутый круг образуя. Кружилась моя голова.
Кончен пробег. Ты умрешь голодающей кровью.
Я разлюбила. Жива.

О, на земле, под землей, оплетенная сетчатой тенью,
что прокричит сирота, чтоб оттянуть переход?
Что отыскать суждено в посмертном пылающем сене?
Только игла уколола … И открывается ход
из глубины. По ступеням
он подымается,

слабое пламя несет …

In Memory of a Friend

Death is a thrifty swallow. For each trash and past it—
for the airborne tremor of wings—she knows the place and taste.
The one you love, grown thinner than a straw,
is caught and hidden by her in a gleaming, weeping bush,
preserved in a terrible nest of Advent torment ...
I'll never see his eyes again, or his lips.

Was it I who foretold immortality? And on the grass outside Moscow
I recall the startled outline of an eye and the retina's gloom.
The note began, "Do you love me?"—and ended, "With love,"
forming a closed circle. My head was spinning.
The race is completed. You'll die of hungering blood.
I fell out of love. Still alive.

Oh, on the earth, under ground, braided with netted shadow,
what will the orphan cry out, to prolong the crossing?
What is he fated to find in the posthumous blazing hay?
Only a needle pricked ... And a path opens
from the depths. Up the stairs
he is ascending,
                    he bears a weak flame ...

2

И вот очнулось нищее страданье,
уже не помня, причитать по ком,
но слабый гласный пар под языком,
растенья слов, излучины молчанья
пугали, оплетали душу — и
гремело небо, осыпались листья,
когда пытались губы о любви
проговорить, а робкий ум — промыслить.

Я поняла, разбившись о края
сосуда боли, кремниевой чаши, —
срастается за ними жизнь моя,
и никогда уже не будет — наша.

Так полузахлебнувшийся зверок,
еще цепляясь за ковчега днище,
не видит, что его звериный бог,
когтями раздвигая воды, ищет …

2

And here beggarly suffering awakens,
already forgetting whom it should lament,
but the weak vocal steam beneath my tongue,
growths of words, the radiance of silence
have frightened, twined around my soul—and
the sky thundered, leaves scattered and fell
when my lips attempted to tell about love,
and my timid mind—to think it through.

I realized, shattered against the edges
of the vessel of pain, the flinty goblet—
my life is knitting together behind them,
and already it never will be ours.

So a half-drowning little creature,
still clutching at the bottom of the ark,
does not see that the god of beasts,
clawing the water apart, is searching for it ...

Декабрь

Окостенелый свет расправлен в декабре.
Леса оголены и встали без дыханья,
и в длинной полынье на утренней заре—
волос безжизненное колыханье.

Угóльного зрачка движенья неживы,
и тени на лице на смертные похожи.
Блестящий низкий лоб и скул монгольских швы—
меж черною водой и ледяною кожей.

Восходит нежный пар—дыханья волокно,
колеблет волосы подводное движенье.
Лежит российская Горгона. Ей темно,
и тонкой сетью льда лицо оплетено,
и ужаса на нем застыло выраженье ...

December

The ossified light is smoothed out in December.
The woods are bared and stand without a breath,
and in the long ice floe in the glow of morning
there is a lifeless flickering of hair.

The movements of the coal-black eye are dead,
and shadows on the face look like a mortal's.
A bright low forehead, seams of Mongol cheekbones—
between the icy skin and the black water.

Tender steam rises—the filament of breath,
her hair stirs with an underwater movement.
The Russian Gorgon lies. It's dark for her,
her face is delicately webbed with ice,
and a look of horror has settled on it …

"И Русского Стиха …"

И русского стиха прохладный, влажный сруб,
звезда под крышкою чудесного колодца …
Смотри, как плещется, кипит у самых губ
вода бескожая, а в гости не дается.

Но если в августе разомкнут небосвод
и мокрой чернотой размыты дали,
кастальская вода в ключах твоих поет
настоем бедности бессмертной и печали.

"And of Russian Verse ..."

1

And the cool, damp log-frame of Russian verse,
a star beneath the lid of a magic well...
Look how it splashes, boils right at the lips,
the skinless water, though it won't come visit.

But if in August the horizon folds open
and wet blackness washes the distances away,
in your springs the Castalian water sings
infused with deathless poverty and sorrow.

2

Ты увидишь монгола в коровьей одёже до пят
и степных мудрецов, испытавших, горят ли божницы.
Отшатнется Рязань, закусив окровавленный плат,
и волчица придет в городище разбитом щениться.

В чем твое искупленье, земля? И отчизной затем
ты зовешься, что емлешь детей своих кости?
Ты—земля без конца, безобразное месиво тел,
но сияют глаза матерей у тебя на коросте.

И за то, что я тоже паду в этот стонущий прах,
и за то, что с рождения в сердце полынное семя,
дай мне только надежду, прощальную соль на губах,
что не станешь ложиться лицом под татарское стремя!

Что болтаю? Какое мне дело до этих людей?
Отпусти меня, мать, позабудь меня, дай мне укрыться!
Только бы не упасть между этих могильных грудей
и водою подземной во чреве не колотиться.

You'll see a Mongol dressed in rawhide down to his ankles
and steppe sages who made sure the icon lamps were lit.
Riazan will recoil from biting the bloodied kerchief,
and the she-wolf will enter the shattered city to whelp.

Where's your redemption, earth? And you call yourself
a fatherland, since you take in your children's bones?
You're an earth without end, a hideous muddle of bodies,
but the eyes of the mothers are shining upon your crust.

And because I too shall fall into that groaning dust,
and because my heart holds a wormwood seed since birth,
give me only the hope, the salt of farewell on my lips,
that you won't lie face-down beneath the Tatar stirrup!

What am I babbling? What do I have to do with these people?
Let me go, mother, forget me, let me go hide!
Just so I won't fall down between these graveyard breasts
and won't beat in the womb like water under ground.

3

Сидят большие мужики,
их бороды клинообразны,
в глазах зимуют светляки,
а руки праздны.

Смоленщина! В моей судьбе—
больные звенья:
ты чернолесье, ты любовь,
погост, где брат мой спит без снов,
и мать—без утоленья.

3

Big peasant men are sitting,
their beards are shaped like wedges,
fireflies hibernate in their eyes,
but their hands are idle.

Smolensk province! In my destiny
there are painful links:
You're broad-leafed forest, and you're love,
a churchyard where my brother sleeps dreamless,
and my mother—without relief.

4

Из ночной столицы кукушка
да клопа жестяное брюшко.
Захолустье. Холуй в дверях
исполкома—дрожащ и перист.
Ключевая ненависть, пенясь,
пребраживается в страх.

И всей-то радости—отросток сна во льду,
под валерианой сердце зарастает,
но кто произнесет анафему труду
и наши судьбы отквитает?
И кто, в крови запястья утопив,
нас вычленит из человечьей хляби,
какая помесь: Соловьев-Алябьев
анафему положит на мотив?

Смотрят ясно и важно дети:
диктатуры грузила, сети
миновали—еще малы.
Сушь. Без хруста изломы тени.
И кипят под окном сирени,
как котлы осадной смолы.

4

From the nighttime city a cuckoo
and a bedbug's tin-can belly.
The back of beyond. The door lackey
at the Exec. Comm. trembles, feathery.
Spring-water hatred, frothing,
re-ferments itself into fear.

And of all joy—sleep sprouts in the ice,
with valerian the heart heals up,
but who'll put an anathema on labor
and settle accounts with our destinies?
And who, dipping their wrists in blood,
will distinguish us from the human abyss,
what a mixture: will Solov'ev-Alyab'ev
set the anathema to this motif?

Children look clearly and solemnly:
the tyrannies of the sinker, the nets
have passed them—they're still small fry.
A drought. Shadows break without snapping.
And the lilacs boil under the window
like kettles of pitch for a siege.

5

Для российской жены на чужбине что станет милей?
Возле сердца горит запыленная веточка дрока,
заучило безличье лицо, но осталась у ней
голубиная завязь зрачка деревенских пророков.

Вот на лавочке в ряд, словно дети, сидят и вещают:
верно, сушь повторится, точнее, дождливый июнь …
Низко-низко над ними кружит, только шапки с голов не сшибает,
дурковатая птица, седой Гамаюн.

Перебилась, прости … Для российской жены вдалеке
есть флакон со снотворным, и капли разбиты в стакане,
Столь безлюдные ночи, что лишь на Каяле-реке
человек помаячит и исчезает в тумане.

Ты снисходишь до нас, о тяжелая пава чужих поднебесий,
говоришь, что Россия на взлете, точнее, мы все прогорим…
И кружит над тобою, как пыль по дорогам безлесий,
столь свободный, столь ароматический дым.

Если сердце закушено, если татарская ртуть
раскатилась по жилам, то нам ли с тобой об обиде?
Под каким бы бетонным надгробьем, в какой бы земле ни уснуть,
эти пажити горя о только бы помнить и видеть!

5

For a woman from Russia abroad what could ever be dearer?
A dusty sprig of gorse burns beside her heart,
her face has learned facelessness, but there still remains
the dove-like seed-case of village prophets' visions.

There they sit in a row on the bench, like children, and prophesy:
the drought's sure to repeat or, instead, a rainy June ...
Low-low above them, all but knocking their hats off,
circles the silly bird, grey-haired Gamayun.

I got side-tracked, excuse me ... A woman from Russia abroad
has a vial with a sleeping draught, drops broken up in a glass,
so deserted the nights that only on the river Kayala
can a person drag on a while and disappear in the mist.

You condescend to us, grand heavy bird of strange heavens,
you say Russia's ascending, or rather, we're all going bust ...
And above you, like dust over roads in forestless places,
there circles so free and so aromatic a smoke.

If the heart's bitten, if the Tatar mercury has trundled
off through the veins, then are you and I to bear grudges?
No matter what gravestone cement or what earth you will sleep in,
these pastures of grief, oh but to remember and see!

Когда на деревню плещет гроза кипятком,
берег разбила река и повалено жито,
бьет Илия-пророк по облакам молотком,
а облака грузны, градом набиты.

Но открывается короб небесных сластей:
поле согреет, лесные гостинцы тешат,
и Богородица нежит небесных детей,
чинит рубахи им, мягкие волосы чешет.

Малым на радость Нисский рисует в полях
скользкий закатный воздух, потные крыши,
как молоком наливается к ночи земля,
месяц прозрачный—и самолет повыше.

~

When a downpour splashes the village like boiling water,
the river has broken its bank and the rye's knocked flat,
the Prophet Elijah hammers on the clouds,
and these clouds are heavy laden, stuffed with hail,

But a box of heavenly treats comes open:
the field warms, the gifts of the forest entertain,
and God's Mother caresses the heavenly children,
she mends their shirts, combs out their soft hair.

For the little ones' joy, in the fields Nissky draws
slippery air at sunset, sweaty roofs,
the earth seems to ripen with milk towards nightfall,
transparent moon—and an airplane higher up.

Стихи сыну

Вечерней влагою полна листва.
На лбу—невидимая паутина.
Легко и сонно падают слова,
которыми укачиваю сына.

Едва пошевелюсь, как тень моя
скользит через дорогу. Там соседи
на лавке … Льется жизнь через края
в томительной и стройной их беседе.

Младенец спит. Он сыт и невесом.
Он муравьям рассыпал погремушки.
Настал тот час, когда особый сон
с усталым телом сращивает душу
бессмертную …
                        В траве ворчит гусак,
сползает паутина на ресницы …

Хозяин—в доме. Бог—на небесах.
И хлебный ангел всей деревне снится.

Verses to My Son

1

The foliage is full of evening damp.
On my forehead an invisible spider web.
Lightly and drowsily fall the words
with which I lull my son to sleep.

If I stir even a little bit, my shadow
slips across the road. There the neighbors
sit on a bench … Life pours over the edges
in their tedious, orderly conversation.

The infant sleeps. He's sated and weightless.
He has scattered his rattles to the ants.
That hour has come when a special kind of sleep
knits the weary body to the immortal
soul …
            In the grass a gander mutters,
the spiderweb slips down onto my lashes …

The master of the house is home. God is in heaven.
And the whole village dreams of the grain angel.

2

Хлебный ангел, ангел снежный, ангел, занятый косьбой,—
все три ангела, три ангела кружатся над тобой.
Опускаются, хлопочут, целый день снуют вокруг,
только крылья разноцветные раскрыты на ветру.

Хлебный ангел месит тесто, затевает пироги,
целый день слышны у печки его легкие шаги,
хохолок мелькнет пшеничный, локоть выпачкан в золе—
ставит квас, качает люльку, чтобы мальчик не болел.

Ангел жатвы и покоса проживает во дворе.
У него лицо и плечи облупились на жаре,
косит сено, возит просо, из рожка поит телят …
Его очи голубые ночью в небесах горят.

Белый ангел, ангел снежный—холоднее родника,
твой высокий трубный голос так понятен старикам!
Что за речи на рассвете ты усталым говоришь?
Чистым снегом засыпаешь, чистой памятью даришь.

Вслед за травами и хлебом наступает время сна:
свет и холод, даль и небо, расщепленные до дна,
слабый шелест, сладкий голос—ангел ледянее льда,
врачеванье легкой болью—всех потерь, всего труда.

2

The grain angel, the snow angel, the angel busy mowing—
three angels, three angels keep on circling above you.
They move lower, bustle, all the day they dash about,
only wings of many colors open on the wind.

The bread angel kneads the dough, he turns to making pies,
all day long you can hear his light steps by the stove,
his wheat topknot flashes, his elbow's smudged with cinders—
he sets the ale out, rocks the cradle, so the boy won't be ill.

The harvest and mowing angel spends life in the yard.
His face and his shoulders have been peeling in the heat,
he mows hay, carts the millet, feeds calves from a bottle …
It is his blue eyes that glow in the skies at night.

White angel, snowy angel—colder than spring water,
your high trumpet voice rings so clear to old people!
What speeches do you utter to the weary ones at dawn?
You cover them with virgin snow, you clear their memory.

After the herbs and bread there comes a time for sleep:
light and chill, sky and distance, split down to the base.
A weak rustle, sweet voice—an angel icier than ice,
the healing by slight pain—of all losses, of all labor.

Судак

Странный пейзаж открывается разуму духом узрящим:
редкий бесцветный кустарник и камень горячий.
Нет, это снег Рождества, белые кровли,
дольний дымок слюдяной, стадо под кровом.
Жирной разводы воды под коромыслом,
бледное масло горит в воздухе чистом.
В иглах, цветах ледяных лба полукружье
детского—через стекло вижу снаружи …
Клавдию голос зовет, и отзовется
звонкий подойник в хлеву, цепь у колодца.

Sudak

1

A strange landscape opens to reason's seeing spirit:
sparse colorless shrubbery and a heated stone.
No, it's the snow of Christmas, the white rooftops,
an earthly micaceous smoke thread, the herd under cover.
The patterns of greasy water beneath the yoke,
pale oil is burning in the clear, pure air.
The childlike forehead's arc is covered in needles,
in icy flowers—through the glass I can see outside …
A voice calls to Claudia, and you hear the response
of a ringing milk-pail in the cowshed, the chain on the well.

2

Нет, это все-таки Крым, Сурожа древнего холм!
На плоскогорье полынь о былом своим твердит языком,
стрелы под нею и кости, давние гости и глина,
впрочем, растет все едино …

Рядом немецкое кладбище; в прах запечен колонист,
рыхлая почва, аптекарь, мята над ним, остролист;
стрелы, костяк, черепица сгорблены в общей земле.
Что тебе делать, живая, на погребальной золе?

Вижу высокий костер, где исчезал Одиссей
(мира окраина. Время спит в штилевой полосе),
жирные хлопья летят, мясо паленое пышет …
Пес его, сидя впотьмах, жадно и жалостно дышит.

2

No, it is still the Crimea, ancient Surozh's hill!
On the plateau wormwood says its word about the past,
arrows lie under it, bones, long-ago guests and clay,
though it all grows the same way …

A German graveyard nearby: the colonist baked into dust,
porous soil, a pharmacist, the mint above him, holly;
arrows, a skeleton, a tile hunching in common ground.
What can you do, living one, on funereal cinders?

I see the high fire where Odysseus disappeared
(the edge of the world. Time sleeps in a zone becalmed),
fatty flakes sail in the air, scorched flesh is blazing …
His hound sits in the dark, greedily and dolefully breathes.

3

Темное, темное тянем питье из остуженной чаши.
Полночи ясный светильник стоит над водою,
радость не вспугнута, тело еще молодое.
Как прохрустят голыши, и песок прошумит по поддонью,
если очнуться, вскочить, если выкрикнуть: «Наши!»

Я начинаю движением губ превращенье созвездий
в шитую знаками шерсть, в письмена золотые,
и запрокинув лицо, напрягая затылок,
ты разбираешь по ним отдаленные вести
из прокаленной земли полуострова—чаши,
из черепичного рая, пыльного сада …
Неисчислимые, длинные очи следят винограда,
как пожухает листва, осыпая ограду,
как зарумянится слива от долгого взгляда.

3

We draw a dark, dark drink from the chilled goblet.
The clear lamp of midnight stands above the water,
joy is not frightened off, your body is still young.
How flat stones will crunch and sand sound along the keel,
if you wake up, jump up, if you cry out: "Ours!"

I begin, with a shift of my lips, the turn of constellations
into wool sewn with signs, into golden characters,
and throwing your face back, straining the back of your head,
you make sense through them of the distant tidings
from the fire-hardened earth of the peninsula—bowls,
from a paradise of tiles, from a dusty garden ...
The innumerable, long eyes of the grapes look to see
how the foliage grows tarnished, scattering on the fence,
how the plum turns rosy from that lengthy look.

4

Теплый, тройного замеса воздух, и свет золотеет.
Сбился туман, развороженный солнечной спицей.
Из Феодосии-Кафы тянется сонная птица,
пристально, умно глядит, а сказать не умеет.

Или душа караима в пестрой повязке?
Или еще генуэзским стеклом отольет оперенье?
Горного воздуха низки, пухлого облака связка,
благоухание детской молитвы вечерней ...

4

Warm, thrice-kneaded air, and the light turns to gold.
The mist has slipped down, roiled by a needle of sunlight.
From Feodosia-Kafa a sleepy bird drags along,
it looks smart and intent, but it cannot speak.

Or is it a Karaite's soul in a colorful headband?
Or will the plumage gleam like Genovese glass?
The bead-strings of mountain air, a plump sheaf of cloud,
the sweet aroma of children's evening prayers …

Жена Лота

—Ты обернешься?

                —Нет.

—Ты обернешься …

                —Нет.

—И в городе своем
увидишь яркий свет,
почуешь едкий дым—
пылает отчий дом.
       О горе вам, сады—
Гоморра и Содом!

—Не обернусь. Святым
дано—соблазн бороть.
По рекам золотым
несет меня Господь.
—По рекам золотым
несет тебя Господь,
а там орет сквозь дым
обугленная плоть.

—О чем ручьи поют?
—Там пепел и зола.
Над ангелом встают
два огненных крыла.

— Они виновны.

                —Так.

—Они преступны!

                —Так.

Lot's Wife

"Will you turn around?"
                              "No."
"You will turn around …"
                              "No."

"And in that city of yours
you'll see a brilliant light,
you'll smell the caustic smoke—
your father's house ablaze.
O woe to you, the gardens—
Gomorrah and Sodom!"

"I won't turn back. The holy
have the gift—to fight temptation.
It is the Lord Who bears me
along the golden rivers."
"The Lord it is Who bears you
along the golden rivers,
but there carbonized flesh
bellows amid the smoke."

"What do the streams sing of?"
"There, there is ash and cinder.
Above the angel rise
two wings made out of fire."

"They are at fault."
                              "It's so."
"They're criminals."
                              "It's so."

На грешной наготе
огня расправлен знак.
Ребенок на бегу—
багровая звезда …
—Ты плачешь?

                    —Не могу …

Всем поворотом:

                    —Да.

On sinful nakedness
the sign of fire is stamped.
A child caught at a run
becomes a crimson star …"
"You're crying?"

                          "I can't bear …"

With her whole turning:

                          "Yes."

~

Век можно провести, читая Геродота:
то скифы персов бьют, то персы жгут кого-то …
Но выцветает кровь. В истории твоей—
оливы шум, крестьянский запах пота.

Мельчает греков грубая семья,
спешит ладья военная в Египет.
Мы горечи чужой не можем выпить,
нам—только имена, как стерни от жнивья,
а посох в те края на камне выбит.

И где она, земля лидийских гордецов,
золотоносных рек и золотых полотен,
где мир—в зародыше, где он еще так плотен,
где в небе ходит кровь сожженных городов,
где человек жесток и наг и беззаботен …

~

You can spend a century reading Herodotus:
Scythians beat Persians, then the Persians burn someone ...
But the blooodstains fade. In your history are
the rustle of olives, the peasant smell of sweat.

The coarse clan of the Greeks grows pettier,
the naval vessel hastens towards Egypt.
We cannot drink up all of a stranger's grief,
we see just names, like stubble after reaping,
and the walking-staff beat out on these lands' stone.

And where is it, land of the arrogant Lydians,
gold-bearing rivers and golden linen sails,
where the world's in embryo, where it's still so dense,
where the blood of burned cities walks around the sky,
where man is cruel and naked and free of care ...

Вот и ты возвращаешься в благословенную землю.
Пахнет воском и вереском в старых московских церквях,
там, где у Богородицы плечи в узорных платках,
где прилежные лица святые к высотам подъемлют,
где багровое золото гневно горит в небесах.

Да, и ты возвращаешься, перегорев до конца,
ничего не жалея из жизни, разменянной мелко.
—Вот—я, наг и безроден ...
                        Материнские плечи померкли,
и печалью полна драгоценная чаша лица.

Возвращаешься в трудный круговорот бытия,
в жернов мельничный ...
                        Гулит вода, уходя из запруды,
мальчик гонит козленка, и мать его шьет у ручья,
и тяжелого света стекает на жернов струя—
все—в начале пути, в ожидании чуда.

So you too are coming back to the blessed land.
The old Moscow churches smell of wax and heather,
there, where the Virgin's shoulders wear patterned shawls,
where the saints lift their diligent faces towards the heights,
where the crimson gold burns wrathfully in the heavens.

Yes, you too come back, having burned through to the end,
with no regret for a life that came down to small change.
"Here I am, naked and homeless ..."
                                    The motherly shoulders darkened,
and the precious vessel of her face is full of grief.

You come back into the difficult whirlpool of Being,
to the grindstone ...
                                    The water gurgles, leaving the mill-pond,
a boy drives a goat, and his mother sews by the stream,
and a ray of heavy light falls upon the grindstone—
everything opens a path, awaiting a miracle.

Марсия дудкой клянусь, Марсия кожей,
тою кифарой, что нынче разбита, увы,—
нет ничего пустотелого слова дороже,
хвойного звука ручья, вечного шума травы.

Детская спесь у сатира—мохнатую голову лавром
он увенчал, и свирель, что Афиною гневно
брошена (ибо игра искажала черты богоравных),
он подобрал и дудит. И рожа его вдохновенна.

Что же—не тем ли мы платим: лица искаженьем и цели,
рабством гордыни, клейменьем любви без ответа—
за мусикийские игры, за хрипловатые трели
дудки богини, с рожденья подобранной где-то?

И воздает Аполлон—за целую жизнь—в перегонку:
мертворожденная кровь стекает сведенною мышцей,
дудка, раздавлена болью, всхрипнет еще еле слышно,
лира звенит из травы—эхо негромко …

В эту судьбу я гляжу и вижу, как каждая капля
крови, упавшей в песок, бормочет и учится пенью,
и повторяется вновь жуткое это сраженье—
звуки небес вперемежку с воплями из живодерни,
дудка в горсти у младенца … Певчество и нетерпенье.

~

I swear by the pipe of Marsyas, the skin of Marsyas,
by that cithara that is broken now, alas—
there is nothing more dear than a hollow word,
the pine-needle stream sound, the grass's eternal noise.

The satyr has a child's arrogance—he has crowned
his shaggy head with laurel, and the reed-pipe that Athena
wrathfully cast down (for playing warped her divine features),
he has picked up, and he pipes. And his snout is inspired.

So what—don't we pay with the same: warped face and intention,
the bondage of pride, the branding of love without answer—
for the Musical games, for the wheezing trills
of the goddess's pipe, picked up somewhere at birth?

And Apollo gives back—for a whole life—in overabundance:
stillborn blood congeals like a cramping muscle,
the pipe, crushed by pain, will wheeze again, barely audible,
the lyre rings out from the grass—a gentle echo …

I look into this fate and I see the way each drop of blood,
fallen into the sand, mutters and learns to sing.
And once again this horrible strife is repeated—
heavenly sounds alternating with cries from the slaughter,
the fife in an infant's fist … Making songs and impatience.

Здесь, где живу и о точило жизни
истачиваю сердце всякий день,
здесь, где со мной умрут мои деревья,
мою деревню оползень накроет,
и жизни след—полировальной тряпкой
дыханья влагу—со стола сотрут,
я так любила, Господи, Твой мир!

Всего родней и ближе поняла
я о Тебе в степи, где травы кровью
вспоили воздух, звезды ... Ночь текла
огромными пространствами. Была
я мельче пыли в вечной этой нови
движения гигантского. Спала—
и вдруг очнулась, зная—в изголовье
два несказанных, радостных крыла!

Here where I live and on life's whetstone
slowly bleed my heart out with each day,
here where my trees will die along with me,
my village will be covered by a landslide,
and they will wipe away life's trace—as a cloth
polishes the damp of breath—from the table,
I loved Thy world, oh Lord, so very much!

Dearest and best I came to understand Thee
in the steppe, where the grasses nourished
the air and stars with blood … Night flowed
just like enormous spaces. I was more fine
than dust in this eternal novelty
of gigantic movement. I was sleeping—
and suddenly awoke, knowing—at the head
of my bed were two ineffable joyous wings!

Вот кольцо с малахитом. И в каждой прожилке—зима.
Я гляжу в эту плоскую твердь, холодея сама—
знал ли ты засыпанье, не чающее воскресенья?
Перетянуты бедра суровою ниткою сна, коченеет язык,
и в гортани черно. И не мой ли счастливый двойник
обретает наутро нестойкое раннее зренье?

А еще в малахите моем незлобивая смерть:
белоглазые щелки и черно-зеленая твердь,
знаки тленья и плесени. Но безупречна огранка.
У моей ли судьбы во все очи лазурь без зрачка?
Щедро дарит она, а в конце—ледяного щелчка,
как ударом ствола добивают подранка.

Перегонкою крови в слова не избегнешь земли,
не взойти к небесам в изумрудной горячей пыли—
только камень и кровь, и спокоен стрелок на охоте …
Я гляжу на кольцо. Сколько жилок белесых пришлось
на зеленое поле—его изглодали насквозь,
как прозрачные черви в своей потаенной работе.

~

Here's a malachite ring. And in every vein there is winter.
I gaze into this flat firmament, growing colder myself—
have you ever fallen asleep, not expecting resurrection?
Hips wound tight with sleep's harsh thread, the tongue goes numb
and it's dark in the larynx. And isn't it my lucky double
who'll obtain in the morning an early impermanent vision?

And in my malachite there is also timid death:
white-eyed slits and a firmament of black-green,
the signs of decay and mold. But irreproachable polish.
Does my fate face in all eyes an azure that's lacking a pupil?
It gives generous gifts, but ends with an icy thwack,
as they finish a wounded bird off with a blow of the barrel.

You can't escape earth by distilling blood into words,
can't ascend to the heavens in burning emerald dust—
only blood and stone, and a calm hunter with a gun …
I gaze at the ring. How many whitish veins have fallen
to the lot of the green field—it's been gnawed right through,
as if by transparent worms at their secretive work.

В любви несчастной есть избыток света
и царственная горечь. Столь нелепы
смиренье, ожиданье и мольбы,
и унижение так театрально—
не уломать, не умолить судьбы.

В любви несчастной есть придонный свет,
и не сорвется одинокий голос,
заслышав отклик. Целый мир, как полость
рапана—моря шум, но моря нет.

О, одиночества голубизна,
чужого счастья рабская галера,
и человек с лицом легионера
все так же снится …

~

In unhappy love there is an excess of light
and regal bitterness. So nonsensical
are meekness, expectation and entreaties
and humiliation's so theatrical—
not to persuade, not to plead with fate.

An unhappy love has a light in the depths,
and the solitary voice will not break,
hearing an answer. The whole world, like the cavity
of a shell—the sea's noise, but there's no sea.

Oh, the sky-blueness of being alone,
the slave galley of someone else's joy,
and the man with the face of a legionary
that I keep seeing in dreams …

Византийская синь. Молочный дым.
Кристаллический иней. Граненый снег.
Голенастым, хмурым и молодым
я запомню тебя навек.
Я запомню сияющий ломкий наст
и утраты свежую полынью:
на Хованском кладбище страшный пласт—
там сховали подругу мою.
Как потом отворялся колодец сна
и лечила звездная немота …
Утешенья вода голуба, черна,
Обручальным золотом повита.

Byzantine indigo. A milky smoke.
Crystalline hoarfrost. Beveled snow.
I'll remember you forever
as long-legged, gloomy and young.
I'll remember the gleaming crisp ice crust
and the fresh open water of loss:
at Khovan cemetery a terrible layer—
there where my girlfriend is buried.
How afterwards the well of sleep would open
and starry silence brought healing ...
The water of consolation is blue, is black,
wrapped round in the gold of Betrothal.

Наши святочные гаданья,
картонный король, валет с алебардой
заслоняют от страха жизни.
Вот шевельнулась смерть на хребте Кавказском,
встала графитной тучей над Украиной,
тычет в затылок: «вести, вестимо, васти …»
и растирает в крошки дешевый ластик,
сотни имен стирая.
В святки раскроем книгу,
распечатаем карты в цветных рубашках—
и парафин в воде, и кофейная гуща
сплавились, слиты в одно: «Сохрани их, Боже!»
Слово в слезах восходит.
Святки. В развале спальни
я и часы наперебой бормочем.
А за окном зима. Под ледяной подошвой
снится реке—крещенской купели прорубь.

Our holiday fortune-telling,
the cardboard king, the jack with his halberd
fence you off from fear of life.
Here death has stirred on the spine of the Caucasus,
has risen in a graphite cloud above Ukraine,
it pokes the back of your head: "news, we inform, known …"
and smears the cheap eraser into scrubbings,
wiping out hundreds of names.
At Christmas we'll open a book,
we'll unseal the cards in their colorful shirts—
and hot wax in water, and the coffee grounds
fuse together, mixed in one: "God preserve them!"
The word ascends in tears.
Christmastime. In the bedroom mess
the clock and I take turns muttering.
And out the window it's winter. Beneath a frozen sole
the river dreams of Epiphany's baptismal font.

Мне никогда не вернуть перепелок в полях
(влажный их куст, возникающий сразу на взлете),
шороха ночью в сарае и—детям на страх—
россказней про кабанов на заросшем болоте.

Бабка учила письму на коротком письме,
путались мамины строчки, и все-то мне снилось:
невод волос ее темных и слово ко мне,
слово любви искалеченным золотом билось.

Старое русло моя заливала судьба,
ствол кровеносный полнился помнящей кровью …
Братьев моих голоса, бабок моих ворожба—
что вы сулили, сойдясь по ночам к изголовью?

~

I'll never manage to bring back the quail in the fields
(their damp bough arising at once as they take flight),
the rustle at night in the barn and—to scare the children—
tale-telling about wild boars in the overgrown swamp.

Granny taught me my letters from an envelope,
mama's lines got mixed up, and I kept dreaming:
the fishing-net of her dark hair and the word to me,
a word of love that struggled in crippled gold.

My destiny flooded over the old channel,
the arterial bole filled up with remembering blood …
My brothers' voices, my grandmothers' magic—
what did you portend, gathered by night at my bed?

Мы выехали из лесу. Вповал
в телеге спали дети. Сонный ветер
распаренные лица обдувал,
и неба край, уже горяч и ал,
сиял сквозь ветви.

Еще к деревьям прирастала тень,
ночная птица медленно летела,
и мальчик мой, похож на всех детей,
зарывшись в сено, спал на животе,
и прядка на виске его вспотела.

Цветущая лесная колея,
тихоня-конь, разморенные дети
и голубое поле льна в просвете …
О будь благословенна, жизнь моя,
за то, что ты дала минуты эти
пронзительного счастья бытия!

We drove out of the forest. In a heap
the children slept in the cart. A drowsy wind
blew all around their sweaty faces,
and the sky's edge, already hot and scarlet,
came shining through the branches.

A shadow grew beside the trees,
a nighttime bird was flying slowly,
and my little boy, like all the children,
burrowed into the hay, slept on his belly,
and a sweaty lock lay on his temple.

The flowering forest cart-track,
the demure horse, exhausted children
and a sky-blue field of flax in a shaft of light …
Oh may thou be blessed, my life,
since thou hast given to me these minutes
of the piercing happiness of Being!

Вот я прямо иду, на север. Морошка, корни,
больно, больно ступать! Болото тебя прокормит.
Затянуло крапивой заброшенный лагерь, вышки.
На Египет спешат эти птицы, из речки вышли.

Оперенный иероглиф летит—а зрачки вдогонку,
вот я прямо, на север, а смерть отошла в сторонку,
сердце ищет смоленских трав—валерианы, мяты.
Духом нищие на земле—перейдя, богаты!

Я богатство свое раздарю, расточу заране,
а болото прокор… А там не ступай—поранит,
а тропинки не бой… Сойди же, о ради Бога!
Слава Господу, призрящему нас на Его дорогах!

~

Here I go straight ahead, northward. Cloudberry, roots,
it hurts, hurts to walk! The swamp will keep you fed.
The abandoned camp's full of nettles, the watch-towers.
These birds hurry towards Egypt, they came from the stream.

The feathered hieroglyph flies—and my eyes follow,
here straight ahead, northward, and death moves off to the side,
my heart seeks the herbs of Smolensk—valerian, mint…
The poor in spirit on earth—passing on, they are wealthy!

I will give my wealth away, squander it in advance,
and the swamp will kee… But don't step there, it'll cut you,
and don't fear the pa… Come down then, oh for the Lord!
Praise be to God, who cares for us on His roads!

Всадник бел на оснеженной горе.
Дрогнет яблоко в кожуре,
зарумянясь на замше перчатки.
Вышли деды: «Здравствуйте, генерал!»
Овчина шапок. «Здравствуйте, генерал!
Будь вам наши яблоки сладки».

Мне приснился Скобелев-генерал,
невысокий утоптанный перевал,
крап кровавый и кремень Шипки.
Турок нам то что твой басмач,
славянин—воитель и бородач—
переможет, конечно, в сшибке.

Заведу избу, а в ней образа,
а под ними картинку—смотреть глазам,
как гарцует Скобелев на лошадке …
Вот и пристань—здравствуйте, генерал!
Коммунисты—слышали, генерал?
Нам былого сумерки сладки.

The horseman's white on a snow-covered mountain.
The apple will quiver in its peel,
showing rosy against his glove's suede.
The grandfathers came out—"Greetings, general!"
Their sheepskin hats. "Greetings, general!
May our apples taste sweet to you."

I had a dream of Skobelev the general,
a low-elevation, trampled mountain pass,
a bloody pattern and the flint of Shipka.
To us a Turk's the same thing as a thug,
the Slav—a bearded warrior—
will prevail, of course, in the clinch.

I'll set up a hut, and inside it the icons,
and beneath them a picture—for my eyes to see
how Skobelev prances on his little horse …
And there's the jetty—greetings, general!
The Communists—have you heard, general?
The twilight of the past is sweet to us.

Родственники

У мамы был любовник. Он приходил
каждый вечер, ее жалея.
Пробираясь по коридору вдоль бочек
с прелой солониной, одичалым пивом,
«Темные аллеи,—бормотал,—темные аллеи …»

Мамин любовник погиб на Дону.
Она молила морфию в аптеке,
грызла фуражку, забытую им …
Его зарыли в песок, вниз лицом.
Кто скажет, сколько пуль спит в этом человеке?

Relatives

1

Mama had a lover. He came over
every evening, feeling sorry for her.
Picking his way down the hall past barrels
of fusty salted meat, of spoiling beer,
"Dark alleys," he would mutter, "dark alleys …"

Mama's lover perished on the Don.
She begged for morphine at the pharmacy,
chewed the army cap he had left behind …
They buried him in sand, face-down.
Who can say how many bullets sleep in that man?

2

Как хорошела в безумье, как отходила
и серебрела душа, втянута небом.
А за вагонным окном и мело и томило
всей белизною судьбы, снегом судебным.

Как хорошела. Лозой восходили к окошку
кофты ее рукава, прозелень глаза …
И осыпалась судьба—крошевом, крошкой.
Не пожила. И не пожалела ни разу.

Родственница. Девятнадцатый год. Смерть в вагоне.
Бабы жалели и рылись в белье и подушке:
брата портрет—за каким Сивашом похоронят?—
да образок с Соловков—замещенье иконе,
хлебные крошки, обломки игрушки …

2

How beautiful she grew in madness, how her soul
would stray and grow silver, drawn in by the sky.
And outside the train window it snowed and wore on
with all the blank of fate, of juridical snow.

How she grew beautiful. Like a grapevine her blouse's
sleeve rose to the window, her eye's green tinge ...
And fate flaked down—in a hash, in crumbs.
She hadn't lived. And didn't regret it once.

A relative. Nineteen-nineteen. Death on a train.
The peasant women took pity, searched her bedding:
her brother's portrait—he's buried by what Sivash?—
and an image from Solovki—substitute for an icon,
crumbs of bread, pieces of broken toys ...

3

Снега равнинные пряди. Перхоть пехоты.
Что-то мы едем, куда? Наниматься в прислугу.
Наголодались в Поволжье до смерти, до рвоты,
слава-те Господи, не поглодали друг друга.

Зашевелились холмы серою смушкой.
Колокола голосят, как при Батые.
На сухари обменяли кольца в теплушке
Зина, Наталья, Любовь, Нина, Мария.

Хлеб с волокном лебеды горек и мылист,
режется в черной косе снежная прядка …
Так за семью в эти дни тетки молились,
что до сих пор на душе страшно и сладко.

3

Low-country locks of snow. The dandruff of infantry.
We seem to be traveling, where? To find work as servants.
We were starving on the Volga, to death, to nausea,
thanks be to God that we didn't gnaw on each other.

The hills began to stir like grey astrakhan.
The bells give voice, as in Khan Batu's time.
Zina, Natalia, Lyubov, Nina and Maria
traded their rings for breadcrusts on the train.

The bread with a thread of goatsfoot is bitter and soapy,
a snowy strand cuts into the black braid ...
In those days aunts prayed for the family so,
that to this day my soul still feels scared and sweet.

4

Хвойной, хлебной, заросшей, но смысл сохранившей и речь
родине среднерусской промолвив «прости»,
я просила бы здесь умереть, чтобы семечком лечь
в чернопахотной смуглой горсти.

Мне мерещилась Курбского тень у твоих рубежей
в дни, когда я в Литве куковала, томясь по тебе.
Ты таких родила и вернула в утробу мужей,
что твой воздух вдохнет Судный ангел, приникнув к трубе.

Ибо голос о жизни Нетленной и Страшном суде
спит в корнях чернолесья, глубинах горячих полей,
и нетвердо язык заучив, шелестя о судьбе,
обвисают над крышами крылья твоих тополей,

Голубиная Книга и горлица, завязь сердец …
Сытный воздух, репейник цветущий, встающий стеной.
Пьян от горечи проводов, плачет и рвется отец,
и мохнатый обоз заскользит по реке ледяной.

4

After saying "forgive me" to my central Russian homeland,
coniferous, fertile, overgrown, but keeping sense and speech,
I would ask to meet death here, to lie down as a seed
in a swarthy, black-ploughing handful.

I thought I glimpsed Kurbsky's shadow at your borders
in the days when I mourned in Lithuania, longing for you.
You bore such heroes and took them back into your womb,
the angel of Judgment will breathe your air, lifting the trumpet.

For the voice of Life Incorruptible and the Last Judgment
sleeps in the pine forest's roots, in the depths of hot fields,
and having learned the tongue somewhat, rustling about fate,
poplars dangle their wings above the roofs,

the Dove Book and turtle-dove, intertwining hearts …
The nourishing air, blooming burdock, stood up like a wall.
Drunk from bitter parting, a father cries and struggles,
and the mossy carts will slide off down the frozen river.

5

«Обоз мохнатый по реке скользил,—твердит Овидий,—
и стрелы падали у ног, а геты пили лед …»
Изгнанничество, кто твои окраины увидит,
изрежется о кромку льда и смертного испьет.

И полисы не полюса, и те же в них постройки,
и пчелы те же сохранят в граненых сотах мед—
но с погребального костра желанный ветер стойкий
в свои края, к своим стенам пустую тень несет.

Нас изгоняют из числа живых. И в том ли дело,
что в эту реку не глядеть, с чужого есть куста …
Изгнанничество, в даль твою гляжу остолбенело,
не узнавая языка. И дышит чернота.

5

"The mossy carts slid down the river," Ovid asserts,
"and arrows fell at their feet, while the Getæ drank ice ..."
Exile, whoever catches sight of your borderlands
will be cut on the ice's edge and drink of death.

And cities are not poles, and they hold the same buildings,
and the same bees will store honey in beveled combs—
but from the funeral bonfire the stubborn longed-for wind
bears empty shadow to its own lands, to its own walls.

We're exiled from the list of the living. And is it because
you can't gaze in this river, or eat from a stranger's bush ...
Exile, I gaze dumbfoundedly into your distance,
not recognizing the language. And blackness breathes.

6

Спим на чужбине родной.
Месяц стоит молодой
над Неманом чистым, над тихой Литвой,
тот же—в Москве и Курске.
Речи чужой нахлебавшись за день
так же, попав в Гедиминову сень,
здесь засыпал Курбский.

Милое дело отчизна—полон,
черный опричник, малиновый звон
во славу Отца и Сына.
Жизнь коротка. И с тяжелой женой
можно заспать на чужбине родной
память. А смерть обошла стороной.
Милое дело—чужбина.

Как образуется ложь на губах?
Слов раскаленных не выстудил страх,
желчь не разъела кристаллов словесных.
Жилиста правда и ломит хребет
кровным. И правда твоя предстает
Курском разбитым, сожженным Смоленском.

«Господи, их порази, не меня!
Господи, этих прости—и меня!
Боже, помилуй иуду, иуду!»
И засыпает в глубоких слезах …
Сердце плутает в литовских лесах,
слово забывши, не веруя в чудо.

Но большеглазых московских церквей
свет ему снится и голос: «Андрей,
зерна—страданье, а всходы—спасенье!»

We sleep in our own foreign land.
The new moon is standing above
the pure river Neman, quiet Lithuania,
the same as in Moscow and Kursk.
After a day choking down foreign speech
just so, in the shadow of Prince Gedimin,
here Kurbsky used to fall asleep.

A sweet thing, the fatherland—captivity,
a black bodyguard, the mellow bells tolling
in praise of the Father and Son.
Life is brief. And with a heavy wife
one can overlay memory in one's very own
foreign land. Whereas death passed him by.
A sweet thing—a foreign land.

How does a lie take form on the lips?
Fear has not cooled down your blistering words,
gall has not corroded the crystals of speech.
Truth is athletic and can break the spine
of your relatives. And your truth rises up
in shattered Kursk, in the ash of Smolensk.

"Lord, smite them, but do not smite me!
Lord, forgive these—and forgive me as well!
God, have mercy on Judas, on Judas!"
And in deep tears he dozes off …
His heart strays in Lithuanian forests,
forgetting the word, not believing the miracle.

But the light of the big-eyed Muscovite churches
appears in his dreams, and a voice: "Andrei,
grains mean suffering, but sprouts—salvation!"

Первый петух закричал вдалеке,
клевера поле в парном молоке,
зерна, прилипшие к мокрой щеке,
и—сквозь зевоту жены—«Воскресенье!»

The first cock has started to crow in the distance,
the clover field is covered in new milk,
grains are adhering to the damp cheek,
and—through his wife's yawns—"It's Sunday!"

А. Сопровскому

Ты прав: расправленный простор,
трава, присоленная снегом,
и в полночь жизни—смутный вздор,
что не излечишься побегом,
судьба … больна … а не страна—
все это было, было, было,
как бы истертое кино
перед глазами зарябило.

По мне же—горсточка тепла,
свободный говор, гонор нищий
и страшная живая мгла,
что за моей спиною свищет,
важней.
　　　　　В любой из наших встреч
сквозь проговорки и усталость—
земная соль, родная речь
тесней смыкается в кристаллы.

To A. Soprovsky

You're right: a space that's been smoothed out,
the grass, salted a bit with snow,
and at life's midnight—some dim nonsense
that you can't be healed by fleeing,
it's fate … it's sick … but not a country—
all that is so, is so, is so,
as if a worn-out movie print
started to flash before your eyes.

I'd say, a little bit of warmth,
free talk, a beggar's arrogance
and the horrible living gloom,
which whistles behind my back,
count more.
              At any of our meetings
through the pronouncements and weariness—
salt of the earth, our native speech
packs still more tightly into crystals.

В воздухе пахнет жильем.
Пани Антося горбится над шитьем,
воздух иголкой ранен, холст пробит через край,
карий и золотой мальчик в ногах играет,
и я говорю: «Голубь, к нам прилетай,
нищему, голубь, подай!»

Время проступит чернью на серебре.
Выйдешь умыться—снег захрустит в ведре.
Как молоком разбавленный крепкий чай,
бурое солнце взойдет и помедлит час,
новые твердь и небо скует мороз—
звон ото льда и звезд.

Так не забудь же мира на трех китах,
темного тела речки в широких льдах,
всех, кто живет под кровлей, и вербы куст,
беды, суеты наши—и эту грусть:
слышать—лепечет небо и дышит наст,
знать, что волхвы пройдут, не окликнув нас.

The air smells of habitation.
Pani Antosia is hunched over her sewing,
her needle wounds the air, pierces the canvas edge,
a hazel and golden boy plays at her feet,
and I say, "Dove, fly to us,
give alms, dove, to the beggar!"

Time will stand out like tarnish on silver.
You go out to wash up—snow squeaks in the bucket.
Like strong tea that is diluted with milk
a brown sun will rise and linger an hour,
the frost will forge a new earth and heaven—
the ringing of ice and stars.

So don't forget the world that rests on three whales,
the dark body of streams clad in wide ice.
all those who live under a roof, and the willow bush,
our misfortunes, our vanities—and this grief:
to hear the sky chatter and the snow crust breathe,
to know that the Magi will pass without calling us.

Зима на убыль. Ветер тянет мыльней,
грязь чавкает со вкусом под ногою,
дрожащее пространство и нагое
для глаз затруднено, преизобильно.
Поэт со мной, москвич с лицом изгоя,
взглянув окрест, проговорил: «Морильня».

Но посмотри: телесность, кротость, страх,
предродовое напряженье воли
я чувствую и в поле, и в холмах.
Как роженица, путаясь в подоле,
земля в своих границах и морях
встречает полдень в крепости и боли.

Поэт застыл с улыбкою слепой,
над нами к небесам восходит птица …
—И наша жизнь,—я говорю,—постой,
как капля хмеля в чаше золотой,
Бог ведает, во что пресуществится
в отчизне милой, родине святой!

Winter is on the wane. The wind seems soapier,
mud smacks tastily beneath my foot,
the space that is trembling and naked
grows difficult for our eyes, overabundant.
The poet with me, a strange-faced Muscovite,
glancing around, spoke up: "A killing field."

But look: corporeality, meekness, fear,
the tension of will before going into labor.
I feel these both in the field and in the hills.
Like a woman in childbirth, tangling in her hem,
the earth within its boundaries and seas
meets the midday in firmness and in pain.

The poet has frozen still with a blind smile,
above us in the sky a bird's ascending ...
"Our life too," I say, "is a rented room,
like a tipsy drop in a golden cup,
God knows how it all will be transformed
in my dear fatherland, my holy homeland!"

Из мира теней, тенет
дому и граду привет,
где месяц и ангел вместе
вплывают в закатный свет.
Латник в часовне спит,
в лавре от свеч тепло.
Мир тебе, гром-гранит,
сонной реки стекло!
И отзовется: «Нет,
нет твоей тени здесь».
—Есть, —отвечаю, —есмь.
Здешней судьбы замес,
полость истлевших лет.

From the world of shadows and snares
greetings to house and city,
where new moon and angel together
swim into the light of sunset.
The knight in the chapel sleeps,
the monastery warm from candles.
Peace to you, thunder-granite,
the glass of a sleepy river!
And in answer it echoes, "No,
you have no shadow here."
"I have," I reply, "I am.
A mixture of local fate,
a hollow of rotted years."

И я сложила песни на закате
непостижимой, незабвенной эры,
как некогда, за два тысячелетья,
певец, клянущий небо и Дунай.
В закате, за последней из диаспор,
где трещины земли курятся серой,
в закате, в ломком зареве небесном,
в пыли, на оконечности земли
что проку сердцу в травах приворотных
и притираньях памяти?
                                    Четыре
стихии первородных обступили,
сминают нас и пробуют на вкус …
Прощай, тетрадка, возвращайся в Томы!

~

I too composed songs as the sun was setting
on an inscrutable, unforgotten era,
as long ago, two thousand years before,
the singer who cursed heaven and the Danube.
At sunset, after the latest diaspora,
where cracks in the earth smolder with brimstone,
in the sunset, in a brittle heavenly glow,
in dust, at the far reaches of the earth
what can the heart do with herbs for love potions
and with lotions for memory?
                                        The four
primeval elements have clustered round,
they crumple us and try us on for taste …
Farewell, notebook, go back into the Volumes!

Как я тоскую по архитектуре житья
послевоенного—под виноградной бетонною гроздью,
где, как зверок на ладони, пригрелась семья,
воздух тайком добывая на черном морозе.
По лихорадящей родине, вынесшей ад—
кровью налит ее сумрак и гноем рассветы,
и перекличка: «убит … виноват … виноват …»,
и запекаются губы стыдом и ответом.

Господи, нас разметало, как мертвый сорняк,
взрывом отбросило, ядом смертей опоило,
из глубины униженья спрошу Тебя так:
– Господи Боже мой, что с моей родиной было?
Что, обернувшись, увижу? Окоп и бетон,
парка победы цветы, черепа и колосья,
голос о маме, о брате, платке голубом
под виноградной бетонною гроздью …

How I long for the architecture of life
after the war, under a concrete bunch of grapes
where, like a critter in the palm, a family sheltered,
getting their air secretly in the black frost.
For the feverish homeland that went through hell—
her twilight is swollen with blood, her dawns with putrefaction,
and the roll-call goes on: "killed; guilty; guilty,"
and the lips crust shut in shame and in response.

Lord, we've been swept aside just like dead weeds,
tossed by explosions, plied with the poison of deaths,
from the depth of abasement I will question Thee thus:
"Oh Lord my God, what happened to my homeland?
What will I see, when I turn? A trench and cement,
the flowers of Victory Park, skulls and ears of grain,
a voice that speaks of mama, of my brother,
a blue handkerchief underneath the concrete grapes …"

Небо помнит больше, чем мы—не бойся.
Вот, разгораясь, ночь выводит на круги
реку великую, стан у берега, струги,
Нерукотворный Спас над порослью войска.

Есть глубиною в сердце—память. Бывало,
снился мне город за частоколом хищным—
этот улус славянский, это гнездовье птичье—
я никогда такою Москвы не знала.

Небо смыкает смерть и свет воедино,
время не все стирает, почва не все укроет.
Древней дорогою, памятью нашей крови—
белые странники в сторону Палестины.

~

Heaven remembers more than we do—don't fear.
There, blazing up, the night brings out into circles
the great river, the camp by the shore, the boats,
the Face of the Savior above the sprouting troops.

There is memory like depth in the heart. It used to happen
that I'd dream of the city beyond the rapacious paling—
this Slav nomad camp, this avian complex of nests—
I never came to know a Moscow like that.

Heaven combines death and light into one,
time can't erase it all, soil can't cover it all.
By an ancient road, by our own blood's memory,
white pilgrims in the direction of Palestine.

Сизый ангел, приведший в Иерусалим,
и такое прозрачное небо над ним,
а крылья его перепончаты.
Что мне с ним передать воспаленной земле,
где мужают ростки на крови и золе?
Нету писем для северной почты.

Разве это расскажешь? Судьба хороша
тем, что мне не должны ни любви, ни гроша
все, с кем в нежити бились, как в неводе,
чешую обдирая, пробилась—и ах!—
здесь мужчины в таких пожилых пиджаках
припадают к портрету Хомейни.

Мы стоим у "Машбира". Дырявый жилет
прикрывает крыло его. Прошлого нет,
все, что прожито—грубо и начерно.
Но усмешка его, словно оклик впотьмах,
словно он прозревает в кривых небесах,
что нам дальше судьбою назначено.

To M. G.

A dove-grey angel, who led the way to Jerusalem,
and so transparent a heaven over him,
and his wings are stretched with membranes.
What must he and I pass along to the fevered earth,
where seedlings grow to manhood on blood and ash?
No letters to mail to the north.

Can this really be narrated? Fate is good
in that I am owed neither love nor coins
by all those whom I struggled beside in torment,
shucking my snakeskin, I broke through—and ah,
here the men dressed in such elderly jackets
press close to the portrait of Khomeini.

We stand at the Mashbir. A vest full of holes
protects his wing. There is nothing in the past,
all that we lived through is a crude rough draft.
But his smirk is like a reply in the darkness,
as if he sees clearly in the crooked skies
what fate has appointed us further in the future.

M. M.

Время чеховской осени, Марк,
для нас—цветов запоздалых.
Еще не вошли во мрак,
вера и твердость, вера и жалость
поддерживают наш шаг.

Я не знаю, как там, а здесь—
пыльные тени солдат Хусейна,
газ отравный, ужас осенний …
И все же ты есть, я есть,
и Иерусалим хрустальный
стекает вниз ручьями огней,
а небо в алмазах отсюда видней,
чем с нашей родины дальней.

Время медленных облаков,
звук струны и луна в ущербе …
Доктор Чехов, не стоило так далеко
заезжать, не стоило знать языков,
чтобы сказать: "Ich sterbe".

To M. M.

It's a Chekhovian autumn, Mark,
for us—of belated flowers.
We still haven't gone into darkness,
faith and firmness, faith and compassion
support our steps.

I don't know about there, but here—
dusty shadows of Hussein's soldiers,
poison gas, the autumn horror ...
And nonetheless you are, I am,
and crystalline Jerusalem
flows downward in streams of lights,
while the diamond-clad sky is more visible
from here than from our distant homeland.

The time of slow-moving clouds,
a snapped string and a waning moon ...
Doctor Chekhov, it wasn't worth
traveling so far, knowing languages
in order to say, "Ich sterbe."

Как, не ударясь в крик—о фанерном детстве,
бетонном слоне, горнистах гипсовых в парке,
творожном снеге Невы, небе густейшей заварки,
о колоколе воздушном, хранившем меня?

Вечером мамина тень обтекала душу,
не знала молитвы, но все же молилась робко,
в сети ее темных волос—золотая рыбка,
ладонь ее пахла йодом … сонная воркотня.

Всей глубиною крови я льну к забытым
тем вавилонским пятидесятым,
где подмерзала кровь на катке щербатом,
плыл сладковатый лед по губам разбитым.

Время редеет, скатывается в ворох,
а на рассвете так пламенело дерзко,
и остается—памятью в наших порах,
пением матери на ледяных просторах,
снежными прядями над глубиною невской.

How, without crying out, about plywood childhood,
the concrete elephant, plaster buglers in the park,
the Neva's ricotta snow, the most thickly-brewed sky,
and about the diving bell that protected me?

In the evening mama's shadow flowed round my soul,
I didn't know prayers, but I still prayed timidly,
a little goldfish in the net of her dark hair,
her palm smelled of iodine … a sleepy grumbling.

With the whole depth of blood I press towards
those forgotten Babylonian nineteen-fifties
where blood ran cold at the dented skating-rink,
sweetish ice swam over my broken lips.

Time grows thinner, rolls up into a mass,
but at dawn it blazed up so audaciously,
and remains—as a memory in our own days,
as a mother's singing on the icy expanses,
snowy tresses over the depths of the Neva.

～

В этом горчайшем парке еще продолжим гулянья.
Столь он премного воспет, что странно,
что до сих пор деревья выбрасывают почки
и на лугах вороны бродят поодиночке.

Сколько я туфель стоптала, твердя о красотах
его—теням экскурсантов. Кто там
выгуливает ежонка у стены Монплезира—
мы с маленьким сыном в юном ветшающем мире.

Боскеты его—гравюры, пруды его—акварели,
ты, ускоряя шаг, не шевельнешь даже пыли,
но мы здесь перекликались и не тенями были,
и среди каменных лиц наши лица не каменели.

В этом горчайшем … помнишь? Сова окликает полночь.
Света его луны не смыть и водой Иордана,
не замутить слезами—но позовешь на помощь,
и он задрожит, выплывая из цветного тумана.

In this most bitter park we will continue strolling.
It is so overpraised—it seems peculiar
that to this day the trees are putting out buds
and ravens wander in the meadows one by one.

How many shoes I've worn down, asserting its beauties
to the shadows of tourists. Who is that there
walking a hedgehog by the wall of Monplaisir—
my small son and I in a youthful decaying world.

Its groves are etchings, its ponds are water-colors,
you, making haste, won't even stir up the dust,
but we called here to each other and were not shadows,
and among the stone faces our faces did not turn to stone.

In this most bitter ... remember? An owl hails midnight.
The light of its moon can't be washed out by Jordan's water,
can't be muddled by tears—but if you call for help,
it will start trembling as it sails out from the colored fog.

Ю. К.

Как ни круто время, но смиренья дряни не принудит выпить,
колокол воздушный есть среди осоки и в реке-полыни.
Слышишь колокольчик, гуканье младенца,

                                    ветерок в картине—
некое семейство зной пережидает на пути в Египет.

Явственно, художник взял сюжет расхожий ради колорита:
кущ черно-зеленых, позолоты неба, красоты пейзажа.
От людей поодаль гладкий серый ослик дремлет без поклажи,
и воды колодезной малость расплескалось у его копыта.

Бедное семейство, оторопь пророчеств, холодок погони …
Беззащитным локтем женщина босая прикрывает сына.
Выпей из следочка, выпей из колодца, выпей из ладони—
прорастет бессмертьем и благою вестью смерти сердцевина.

Мне ли не понятно? На сердце разрыва зарастет мета,
сухожилья жизни в судороге. Нечем надышаться вволю…
Но рассвет в пустыне, из кустов дрожащих—

                                    столп седого света,
колокол воздушный—глубже горизонта, шире нашей боли,
ярче наших судеб, Юрий и Татьяна и Елизавета!

To Y. K.

The harshest times can't force you to drink down the drivel of humility,
there is a diving bell in the sedge and in the wormwood-river.
You hear a jingling bell, an infant's gurgle,

a breeze in the picture—
some family is waiting out the heat on the way to Egypt.

Clearly, the artist chose a common theme for the local color:
the black-green tree-crests, the gilded sky, the landscape's beauty.
Away from the people a smooth grey donkey is dreaming without his load,
and the well's water has splashed out a little beside his hoof.

A poor family, the shock of the prophecies, the chill of pursuit …
The barefoot woman protects her son with a defenseless elbow.
Drink from the footprint, from the well, from the cupped palm—
the pith of death will sprout into immortality and glad tidings.

Could I not understand this? The rupture's scar will heal on the heart,
the tendons of life are in spasm. There is nothing to breathe freely.
But desert dawn, from trembling bushes—

a pillar of gray-haired light,
the diving bell is deeper than the horizon, broader than our pain,
more vivid than our fates, Yuri and Tatiana and Elizaveta!

В. Родионову

Всхлипнуть, припасть к офицерской шинели—
особый колониальный восторг.
Запад есть Запад, а это Восток.
Видишь, куда мы с тобой залетели?
Здесь застоялся воздух знакомый
пятидесятых, повернутых вспять.
Заповедник детства.

                       Опять, опять
апельсином и золотом пахнут погоны
на кителях молодых отцов.
Как много нас за столом, как тесно!
Сон младенчества. Клан родовой
сомкнут, как крона над головой
вечного дерева. Запах его телесный.

Не просыпаться. В губах матерей
вкус серебра и мяты.
Как бессмертны и как богаты
мы были любовью их …
Нас уносили в сон, в темноту:
очнешься—кругом пустыня в цвету,
тихое пение за стеною—
о ямщике, что клонится в снег,
о роднике, где горячий свет
над ледяною водой живою.

To V. Rodionov

To sob, to press close to an officer's greatcoat—
this is a certain colonial delight.
West is West, whereas this is the East.
Do you see where you and I have wound up?
Here it is that the well-known air went stagnant
as the fifties turned back on themselves.
The nature preserve of childhood.
                                        Again, again
the epaulets smell of oranges and gold
on the young fathers' army jackets.
How many of us at table, how crowded!
A dream of infancy. The clan of relatives
draws close, like a crown above the head
of an eternal tree. Its smell is like flesh.

Not to wake up. On mothers' lips
the taste of silver and mint.
How immortal and how wealthy
we were through their love ...
They carried us off to sleep, in the dark:
you'd wake up with the desert in flower all around,
soft singing on the other side of the wall
about the coachman who tips into the snow,
about the spring where there is a burning light
above the icy living water.

Света холсты на асфальте сыром,
облако пара, как над котлом,
в древнем разломе Геены:
иллюзион там и кладбище роз.
Иллюзион … И по коже мороз—
знаем мы эти виденья.

Что же захватит с собой впопыхах,
в иерусалимский пылающий мрак
новый пришелец, вступая?
Каплей рубинового стекла
он на холме. И подвижная мгла
плотно его обтекает.

Лица любимых? Их не разглядит.
Сонную воду, зернистый гранит,
серую розу из Блока?
«Степь, мол, кругом …» или «смерть, мол, кругом …»—
что он бормочет в безумье своем—
не разобрать издалека.

Мускулы снега в пространстве степей,
узкое небо, стеклянный репей,
сливочный свет снегопада,
песни обрывок, оскому во рту,
первый младенческий крик в темноту,
больше не надо, не надо …

~

Canvases of light upon the damp asphalt,
a cloud of steam, as if over a kettle,
in the ancient cleft of Gehenna:
an illusion is there and a graveyard of roses.
Illusion … And a chill on the skin—
we are familiar with these apparitions.

What does the newcomer grab in his haste
to bring along, as he first steps into
the blazing gloom of Jerusalem?
He is on the hill like a drop of ruby-
colored glass. And the mobile haze
is flowing thickly around him.

The faces of loved ones? He can't see clearly.
The sleepy water, the kerneled granite,
a gray rose taken from Blok?
"Steppe, say, all round …" or "death, say, all round …"—
what he is muttering in his madness
you can't make out from a distance.

Muscles of snow in the steppe's expanse,
a narrow sky, burdock-weed of glass,
the creamy light of the snowfall,
a fragment of song, bitter taste in the mouth,
the first cry of an infant in the darkness,
please don't any more, please don't …

Это почти из романа: ставни скрипят,
и уголь подходит к концу в затяжную зиму,
и лечу я соринкой—во тьме, слепоте, наугад
по заснеженному Иерусалиму.
Это почти из Диккенса: Новый Свет,
семейный очаг, любовь подростка, смятенье …
Между землей и небом—лучшей из скреп
золотая наука смиренья,
когда даруется зрение шире и чище—снег,
и смирение учит, баюкает, утешая,
и хрусталю и камню твоим во сне
«Иерусалим, —шепчу я, — Иерушалаим …»

~

It's like something from a novel: shutters creak,
and the coal running low as winter drags on,
and I fly like a dust-speck—in the dark, blind, at random
through snow-covered Jerusalem.
It's like something from Dickens: the New World,
the family hearth, adolescent love, confusion ...
Between earth and heaven—as the best of braces
the golden science of humility,
when you're given vision more broad and pure—the snow,
and humility teaches, sings lullabies, comforting,
and to your crystal and stone, in a dream,
"Jerusalem," I whisper, "Yerushalayim ..."

Все отнимается, все, чем душа жила.
Друзья и города уже почти не снятся,
и как вернуться мне и чем мне оправдаться?
Чужую жизнь прожив, перегорев дотла,
несчастною рукой к их стенам прикасаться.

Мы подымались в ночь из глубины.
Тяжелый свет всходил по вертикали
к высотам города, где нас почти не ждали,
и были голоса едва слышны:
«О, помнят ли о нас или, как мы, устали?»

И я входила в дом, в печальное тепло,
и в долгую любовь, где все непоправимо …
Но мой Господь достиг Иерусалима!
Я видела, как горизонтом шло,
гремело облако серебряного дыма.

~

It's all taken away, all that the soul lived by.
Already I hardly dream of friends and cities,
how I could return and what could justify me.
Having lived someone else's life, burned to the ground,
to reach for their walls with an unhappy hand.

We climbed up into the night from the depths.
A heavy light arose along the vertical
to the city heights, where they almost didn't expect us,
and the voices were barely audible:
"Oh, do they remember us, or are they tired as we are?"

And I went into the house, into the sorrowful warmth,
and into long love, where nothing can be repaired …
But my Lord did make his way to Jerusalem!
I saw the way a cloud of silver smoke
moved and thundered along the horizontal.

В кислородном морозе пьянящей любви
вижу губы, широкие очи твои,
и душа просыпается в боли.
И не хочется ей возвращаться на круг—
в наваждение слов и смыкание рук,
в кочевое сиротство неволи.
Но она, задыхаясь от нежности, пьет
этот яд ледяной, этот жалящий мед,
расставания мертвую воду,
и на оклик встает, и покорно идет,
и не помнит уже про свободу.
Что за боль! Только в юности можно стерпеть
это жженье, в крови растворенную медь,
но вдыхая осеннее пламя,
я не знала, что не заговорены мы
от подземного жара, провидческой тьмы
и от нового неба над нами.

In the oxygen frost of intoxicating love
I see your lips, your wide-open eyes,
and my soul awakens in pain.
And it doesn't want to turn back around—
to the verbal delusions and closing of arms,
to bondage's wandering orphanhood.
But, choking from tenderness, it drinks
this icy poison, this honey that stings,
the dead water of separation.
It stands at the call, and submissively goes,
and already forgets about liberty.
What pain! Only in youth can one suffer
this burning, this copper dissolved in the blood,
but inhaling the flame of autumn
I didn't know that we weren't enchanted
against undergound heat, prophetic darkness,
and against the new heaven above us.

Дом в Крыму

Короста соли. Корка над свежей болью.
Кровь винограда за грубой корой
лозы. Каждой весной

                    так открывался Крым.

И я не знала тогда, вдыхая
роз запекшихся аромат,
запах граната сладкий,
что за калиткой—

                Калинов мост.

В прибое—пепел сожженных звезд,
гор омертвелые складки—
это черта, за которой несть
ничего из любимого нами здесь.

Нас уже больше на той стороне,

                         чем на этой.

Доктор Леонтьев опять со своим лазаретом
в пекле гражданской …

                Я знала его стариком.

Я любила его. Осыпается дом,

                    расклеванный ветром.

Нас уже больше на той …

             За Калинов мост

по мертвой воде,

              оскальзаясь о камни Стикса,

каждый сон возвращаюсь

                на дальний погост,

в мокрой траве по пояс. И поют мне птицы
в Иерусалиме о Киммерии-Крыме,
о том, что сроднясь,

            не могу проститься.

The House in the Crimea

A scab of salt. A crust over fresh pain.
The blood of grapes beneath the rude bark
of the vine. Each spring
                  Crimea would open like that.
And I didn't know then, inhaling
the fragrance of clotted roses,
the pomegranate's sweet smell,
what lay past the gate—
                  the Kalinov bridge.
Ashes of burnt-out stars in the surf,
the stiff pleats of the mountains—
this is a line past which no thing
that we loved here endures.

There are more of us now on that side
                       than on this.
Doctor Leontiev is with his field hospital
in the scorched civil hell ...
                 I knew him as an old man.
I liked him. The house is crumbling,
                pecked by the wind.
There are more of us now on that ...
               Past the Kalinov bridge
over dead water,
          on the slippery stones of the Styx,
in every dream I return
            to the distant churchyard,
wet grass to my waist. And the birds in Jerusalem
sing to me about Cimmeria-Crimea,
about how, now that I am a relation,
             I cannot say farewell.

[117]

То была роза, в которую я влюбилась,—
декабрьская роза.

        Когда говорим «Эдем»,
мы в наших снегах представляем сад
роз в декабре. Я срываю декабрьскую розу,
подобную тем.
Да, когда говорим «Эдем»,
мы в наших снегах представляем дол,
оливой и лавром заросший до плоских небес.
Олень, запутавшийся рогами в розах,
ягненок, лев …

        Ни воздыханий, ни слез.

На той стороне оврага, за головами роз
дол Аялона грубый, как парусина
с тех пор, как солнце Иисуса Навина
оплавило край его. И кровью истек
пылающий городок за стенами из рафинада.
Горы людей, ослов, коз …

          Кровь выпущена как надо.
Нет, декабрьская роза, Эдем не волшебный сад.
На подошве праха его холмы, на подкладке крови—
все, как в наших снегах, но только древнее стократ,
и ржавчиной смерти деревьев забрызганы кроны,
и декабрьская роза, тугая как Божий свиток,
как гнев Господень—на сердце ложится мне.

To A. V.

It was a rose with which I fell in love—
a December rose.
                    When we say "Eden,"
we in our snows envision a garden
of roses in December. I pick a December rose
resembling those.
Yes, when we say "Eden,"
we in our snows envision a vale
with olive and laurel grown up to the level skies.
A deer whose horns are tangled in roses,
a lamb, a lion …
                    No lamentations, no tears.

On that side of the gully, past the roses' heads
the vale of Ayalon is as rude as canvas
since the days when the sun of Joshua
melted its edge. And the blazing city
flowed with blood behind walls of lump sugar.
Mountains of people, donkeys, goats …
                    Blood let aplenty.
No, December rose, Eden is no magic garden.
Its hills rest on soles of dust, on a lining of blood—
just like in our snows, only a hundredfold more ancient,
and the trees' crowns are sprinkled with a rust of death,
and the December rose, taut as God's scroll,
as the Lord's wrath—lies down upon my heart.

Сколько горя, сколько черной боли
приняла я в городе Петровом.
Греемся на пепелище старом,
плачемся на пепелище новом.
С нежностью и тайною оглядкой,
чужестранка в этом мире сиром,
узнаю потемкинские пятки
у атлантов, гениев, кумиров …
Но когда у Ксении Блаженной
у ее часовни жду рассвета,
жено, о блаженнейшая жено—
сколько счастья было, сколько света!

~

How much sorrow, how much sooty pain
did I take up in Peter's city.
By the old fireside we warm ourselves,
by the new fireside we lament.
With tenderness and a secret glance backwards,
an alien woman in this orphaned world,
I recognize the Potemkin heels
of all the heroes, geniuses, and idols ...
But when beside St. Xenia the Blessed,
at her chapel I await the dawn,
woman, o most blessed among women—
how much happiness was there, how much light!

~

Вы мне ворожите, родные города,
там созревает жизнь, как семечки, тверда,
ты—Вязьма сладкая, ты—брошеный Саратов,
где солнечные дни и пыльные закаты,
где я не поселюсь, наверно, никогда.
В который раз мне видится, как дед,
надев очки, листает книгу рода
(он умер до войны),

он ищет след
моей судьбы—но нет меня, но нет!
Я пустотой страницы много лет
бреду, как по пустыне в дни исхода.

~

You work magic on me, familiar cities,
life ripens there, firm as sunflower seeds,
you—sweet Vyaz'ma, you—abandoned Saratov,
where there are sunny days and dusty sunsets,
where I will probably not resettle, ever.
How many times I've seen the way grandfather,
putting his glasses on, leafs the family book
(he died before the war),

                          he seeks the trace
of my destiny—but I am not there, I'm not!
For many years I've wandered on the empty page,
as if through the desert in the days of exodus.

Сердечный перебой от боли, не от грусти,
и под ногами дерн так прочен и так груб.
Где влажный куст ручья, где разветвленье устьев,
где запах ночи, лепесток у губ?
Когда я почала железную ковригу?
А помнишь крупный шрифт поэмы о Петре
и детства круглый свет—под лампой зрела книга
и нежной желтизной мерцала на столе.
Колесный перестук сливается с «Полтавой»:
полки, и взрытый прах, и пылкий Шлиппенбах …
И нить моей судьбы вплелась в судьбу державы,
оставив вкус железа на губах.

My heart skips a beat from pain, not sadness,
and under my feet the turf is so firm and rude.
Where is the stream's damp bush, where the branching estuaries,
where is the scent of night, a petal at the lips?
When did I begin to eat the iron loaf?
And remember the large print of the poem on Peter
and childhood's round world—the book ripened under the lamp
and flickered with tender yellow on the table.
The rhythm of wheels flows together with "Poltava—"
the regiments, ploughed-up dust, ardent Schlippenbach …
And my fate's thread wove into the nation's fate,
leaving the taste of iron on my lips.

Ветер в конце столетья
все грубей и жесточе,
счастлив тот, кто не хочет,
может не замечать, как калечит
все, что мы надышали, сплели—
ледяное пространство вод и земли
бесплодно, как при потопе.
Нас снимают слоями,
как в лихолетье солому с крыш.
Пахнет потом и серой.
Ветер роет пыль пепелищ,
и ночами в бреду твердишь:
—Дай, мне, Господи, веры!

The wind at the century's end
is more and more coarse and cruel,
happy the one who doesn't want,
who can not notice how we're crippled
by all we inhaled, wove together—
the icy space of earth and waters
is fruitless, as if in the flood.
We are taken off in layers,
like straw from the roof in a famine.
It smells of sweat and brimstone.
Wind stirs the dust of the fireplaces,
and at night in delirium you repeat,
"Grant me faith, oh Lord!"

Notes

"And of Russian Verse …"

Anathema—a curse that causes its object to be excluded from a community of religious believers.

Solovyov-Alyabyov—V. Solov'ev-Sedykh was a popular Soviet composer; A. Alyab'ev a nineteenth-century Russian compose, author of the art song «Соловей» ("The Nightingale").

Gamayun—a bird in Russian folklore, said to foretell the future.

Kayala—the river by which the armies of Rus' were defeated by the Polovetsians in the late 12th century, in "The Lay of Igor's Campaign."

Grand heavy bird—in the original, a peahen.

"When a downpour splashes …"

Nissky—Russian landscape artist Georgii Nissky (1903-1987).

Sudak

Surozh—the ancient name for the Crimean city Sudak.

During the reign of Catherine the Great, a large number of ethnic Germans settled in the south of Russia, maintaining their distinct language and customs.

Kafa—the ancient name of the Crimean city Feodosia.

Karaite—a member of an Eastern European Jewish sect that rejected the Talmud.

"I swear by the pipe of Marsyas …"

Marsyas—in Greek mythology, a shepherd who found the flute Athena had thrown away and challenged Apollo to a musical contest. Apollo won and flayed Marsyas alive as punishment.

"Our holiday fortune-telling …"

Cards, hot wax (poured into water to form a shape as it cools and hardens), coffee grounds—all traditional means for telling fortunes.

Baptismal font—a hole is cut through the frozen ice on rivers in traditional Orthodox celebration of the holiday of Epiphany («крещение» means "baptism").

"The horseman's white …"

Shipka—a mountain pass between Bulgaria and Turkey, site of a battle in 1877 during the Russo-Turkish War.

«басмач»—a word used by Russians to describe Central Asian (usually Turkic) peoples rather than Turks proper.

Relatives

Sivash—a stagnant body of water, once part of the Black Sea, in Crimea; near some of the final battles between the Red and White Armies in the Russian Civil War, 1918-1921.

Solovki—a venerable Russian monastery on the sub-Arctic Solovetski islands in the White Sea. By 1919, the monastery was closed, and it became an early "island" in the Soviet Gulag.

Khan Batu (d. 1255)—a leader of the Mongol invasion of Rus'.

Andrei Kurbsky (1528-1583)—first a general of Ivan the Terrible, then (living in exile in the Polish-Lithuanian duchy) his bitter enemy and polemicist.

Gedimin (or Gedymin)—14th century Lithuanian prince who eventually ruled parts of Belarus and some western East Slavic territories.

Oprichnik—a member of the squads of enforcers or private army formed by Ivan the Terrible, which tormented many civilians and contributed to the social breakdown of the Time of Troubles.

«Воскресенье», 'Sunday,' comes from the word for resurrection, «воскресение», though the two are spelled slightly differently. This poem should call on both meanings.

"The air smells of habitation …"

Pani—the Polish equivalent of "Mrs." or "ma'am."

"How I long for the architecture of life …"

«Зверок» is an old-fashioned, folk form suggesting a dear little critter.

Recalling a well-known Soviet WWII song whose chorus refers to the "familiar light-blue handkerchief" of a girl waving good-bye to her beloved as he leaves for the front and likely death.

"Heaven remembers more than we do …"

«Нерукотворный Спас»—Literally, the "Savior Not Made by Hands," a traditional Orthodox icon based on the Byzantine legend of

King Abgar, who was healed by an image made when Christ pressed his face into a linen towel. This differs from the tradition of "Veronica's Veil" in the West, though both images were created without artistic implements.

"A dove grey angel …"

Ayatollah Khomeini—Iranian religious and political leader (died in 1989, not long before Ignatova's arrival in Israel).

The Mashbir a supermarket in downtown Jerusalem.

"It's a Chekhovian autumn …"

A reference to Chekhov's 1882 play, «Цветы запоздалые» ('Belated Flowers'), about a doctor who treats a woman with tuberculosis. Their love begins too late, as she is already seriously ill.

"Ich sterbe" (*I am dying*)—Anton Chekhov ("Doctor" because of his medical education) died of tuberculosis in 1904 in Badenweiler, Germany. The snapped string is from a scene in his play "The Cherry Orchard."

"In this most bitter park …"

Monplaisir—"my pleasure" in French, a palace built for Tsar Peter I ("the Great") in the early 18th century, in the summer vacation town of Petrodvorets (Peterhof), near St. Petersburg.

"Canvases of light upon the damp asphalt …"

«Степь да степь кругом»—a late nineteenth-century Russian art song.

"My heart skips a beat from pain …"

In the Russian fairy tale "The Feather of Finist, Bright Falcon" the heroine learns from an old woman that she will find her lost love only after gnawing away three iron loaves and wearing out three iron staves and three pairs of iron boots. (She does gnaw and wear through them and finds him.)

"the poem on Peter"—Pushkin's poem "Poltava," identified by title a few lines later.

The Score of the Game
Tatiana Shcherbina
Translated by J Kates

Shcherbina emerged in the early 1980s as a spokesperson for the new, independent Moscow culture. Her poetry is now widely published in both established and experimental journals at home and abroad. Shcherbina's poetry blends the personal with the political, and the source for her material is pulled from classical literature, as well as French and German cultural influences.

128 pages / Paper (0-939010-73-9) $12.95

A Kindred Orphanhood
Sergey Gandlevsky
Translated by Philip Metres

An integral member of the Seventies Generation who, despite their relative cultural obscurity or, perhaps, precisely because of their situation as internal émigrés, forged new directions in Russian poetry.

"Out of the Rubik's Cube of Russia rise the complex strains of Sergey Gandlevsky ... superb translations that uncannily make the Russian ours." —ANDREI CODRESCU

136 pages / Paper (0-939010-75-5) $12.95

Lions and Acrobats
Anatoly Naiman
Translated by Margo Shohl Rosen and F.D. Reeve

Anatoly Genrikovich Naiman, poet, novelist, critic and literary translator, was born in 1936 into a family of followers of Tolstoy. Having studied as an enginer, he became one of the Leningrad group of young poets (including his friend Joseph Brodsky) around Anna Akhmatova, whose literary secretary he became from 1962 until her death in 1966, and about whom he wrote the invaluable and popular memoir, *Remembering Anna Akhmatova*. In 2001 two of his novels (most recently *Sir* in 2001) was short-listed for the Russian Booker Prize.

128 pages / Paper (0-939010-82-8) $14.95